PIANO • VOCAL • GUITAR

KE$HA ANIMAL

ISBN 978-1-4234-9890-2

HAL•LEONARD®
CORPORATION
7777 W. BLUEMOUND RD. P.O. BOX 13819 MILWAUKEE, WI 53213

Visit Hal Leonard Online at
www.halleonard.com

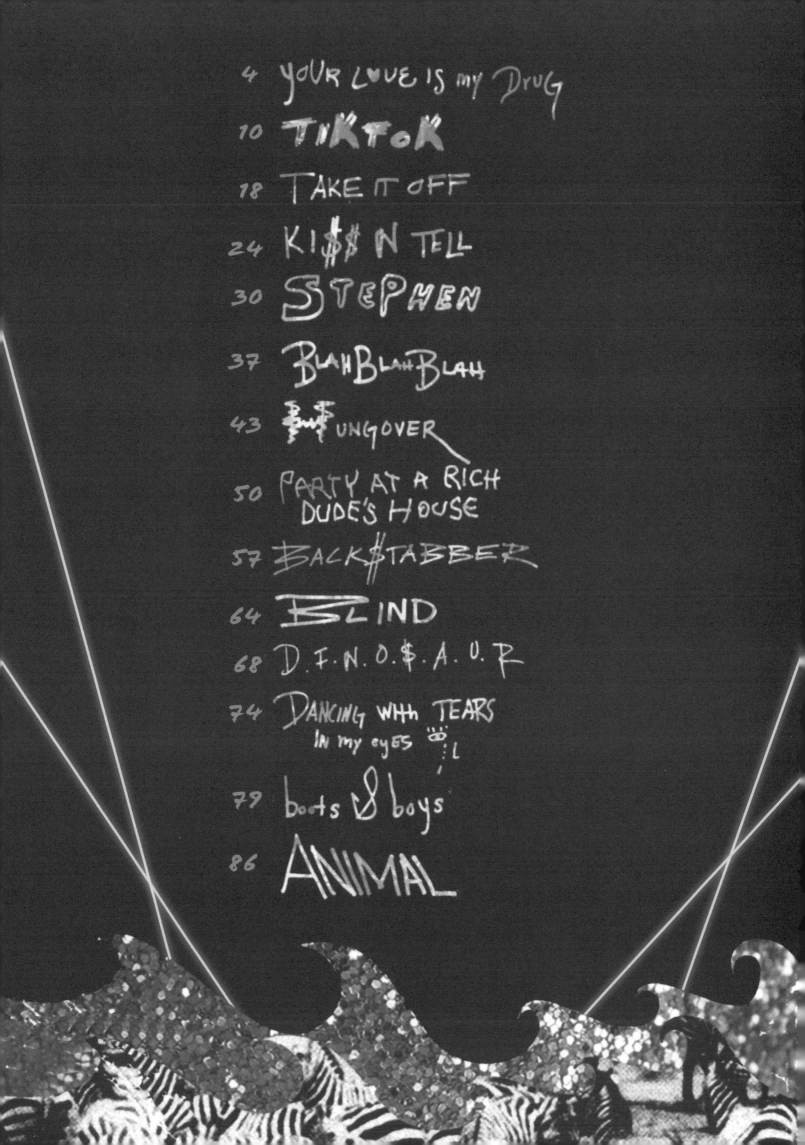

YOUR LOVE IS MY DRUG

Words and Music by KESHA SEBERT,
JOSHUA COLEMAN and PEBE SEBERT

Dance Pop

Maybe I need some re- hab
Won't lis- ten to an- y ad- vice;

or may- be just need some sleep.
Mom's tell- ing me I should think twice.

I got a sick ob- ses- sion,
But left to my own de- vic- es,

I'm see- in' it in my dreams.
I'm ad- dict- ed. It's a cri- sis.

I'm look- in' down ev- 'ry al- ley,
My friends think I've gone cra- zy,

* Recorded a half step higher.

TIK TOK

Words and Music by KESHA SEBERT,
LUKASZ GOTTWALD and BENJAMIN LEVIN

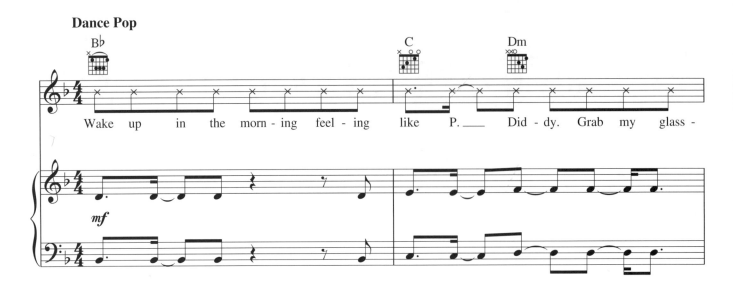

Wake up in the morn-ing feel-ing like P.___ Did-dy. Grab my glass-

es, I'm out the door, I'm gon-na hit this___ cit-y. Be-fore I

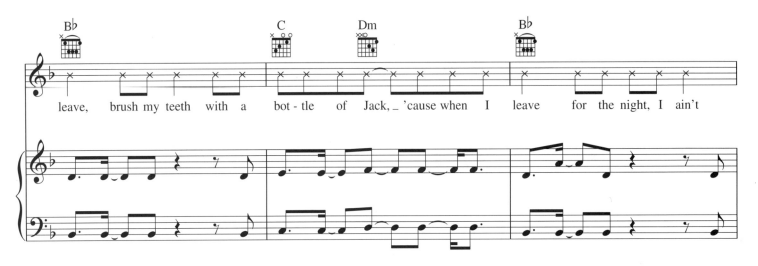

leave, brush my teeth with a bot-tle of Jack, _ 'cause when I leave for the night, I ain't

TAKE IT OFF

Words and Music by KESHA SEBERT,
LUKASZ GOTTWALD and CLAUDE KELLY

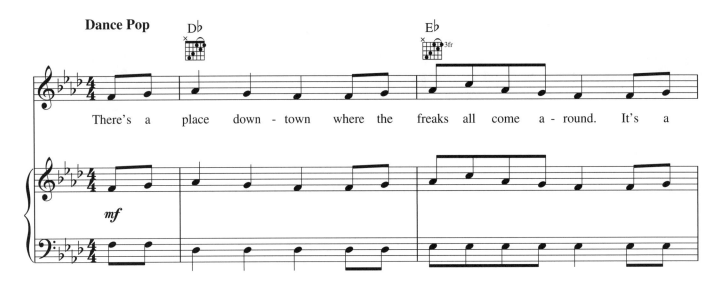

There's a place down-town where the freaks all come a-round. It's a

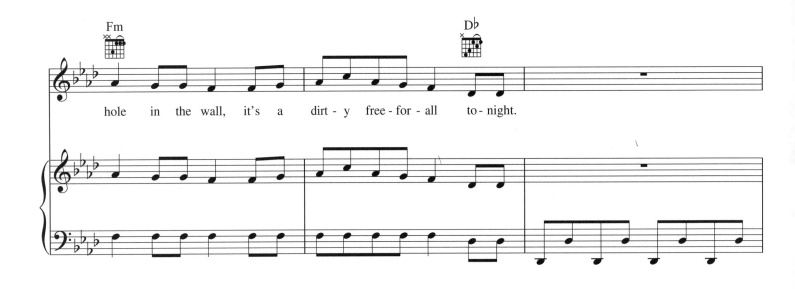

hole in the wall, it's a dirt-y free-for-all to-night.

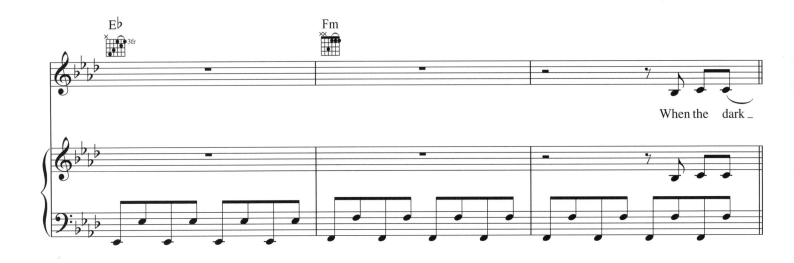

When the dark

KI$$ N TELL

Words and Music by KESHA SEBERT,
LUKASZ GOTTWALD, MAX MARTIN
and JOHAN SCHUSTER

STEPHEN

Words and Music by KESHA SEBERT,
OLIVER LEIBER, PEBE SEBERT
and DAVID GAMSON

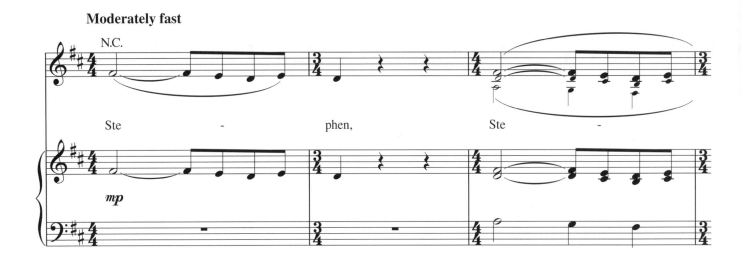

Ste - phen, Ste -

- phen, _ why _____ won't you call me? Ste - phen,

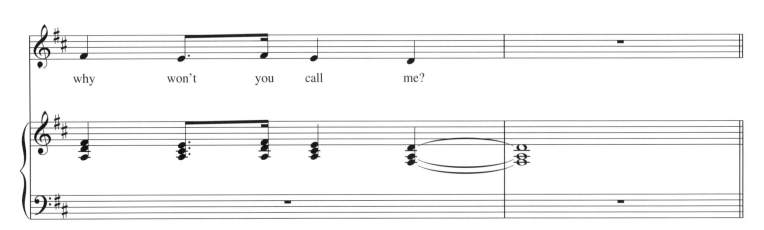

why won't you call me?

BLAH BLAH BLAH

Words and Music by KESHA SEBERT,
BENJAMIN LEVIN, SEAN FOREMAN
and NEON HITCH

Dance Pop

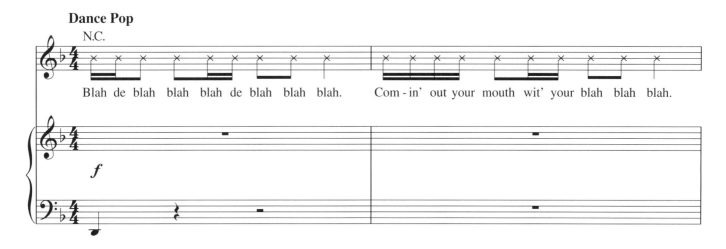

Blah de blah blah blah de blah blah blah. Com-in' out your mouth wit' your blah blah blah.

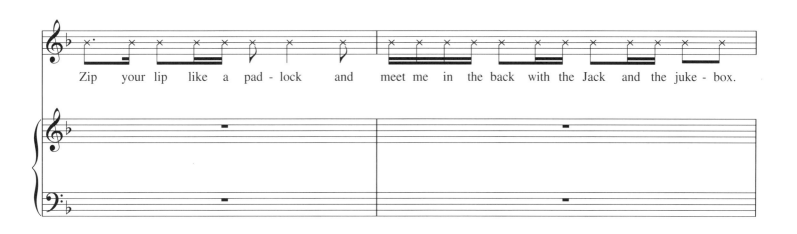

Zip your lip like a pad-lock and meet me in the back with the Jack and the juke-box.

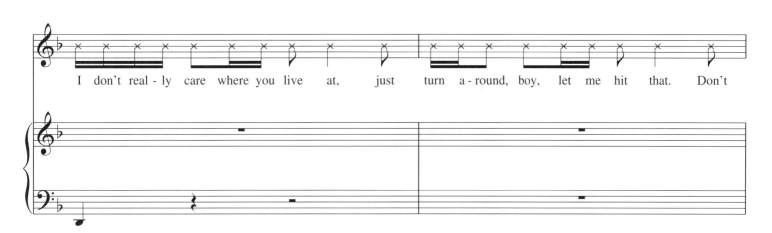

I don't real-ly care where you live at, just turn a-round, boy, let me hit that. Don't

HUNGOVER

Words and Music by KESHA SEBERT,
LUKASZ GOTTWALD, MAX MARTIN
and JOHAN SCHUSTER

Rhythmic Ballad

And now the sun is ris - ing, and now the long _____ walk _ back home, _____
E - ven my dirt - y laun - dry, ev - 'ry - thing _ just smells _ like you, _____

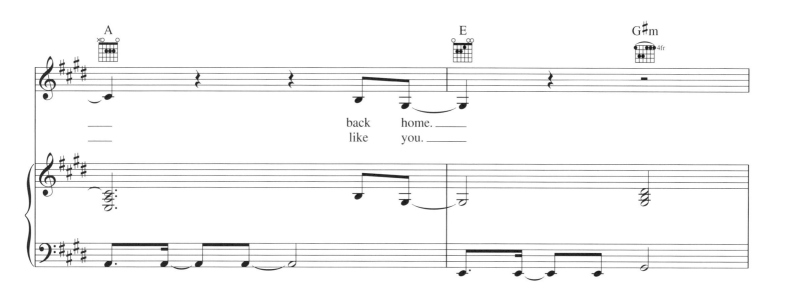

_____ back home. _____
_____ like you. _____

There's just so man - y fac - es, but no one I need to know, _____
And now my head is throb - bing, ev - 'ry song is out of tune, _____

PARTY AT A RICH DUDE'S HOUSE

Words and Music by KESHA SEBERT,
JOHAN SCHUSTER and BENJAMIN LEVIN

BACK$TABBER

Words and Music by KESHA SEBERT,
MARC NELKIN, DAVID GAMSON
and JON INGOLDSBY

Up-tempo groove

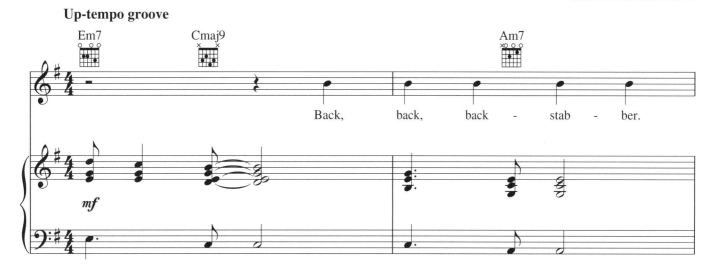

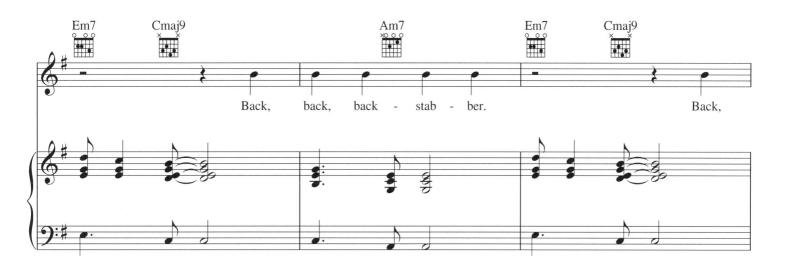

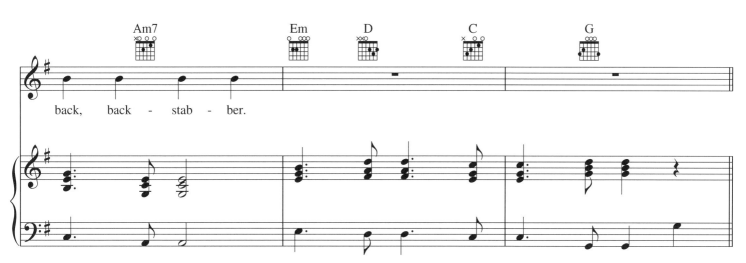

BLIND

Words and Music by KESHA SEBERT,
LUKASZ GOTTWALD, BENJAMIN LEVIN
and JOSHUA COLEMAN

D.I.N.O.$.A.U.R

Words and Music by KESHA SEBERT,
MAX MARTIN and JOHAN SCHUSTER

Jungle beat

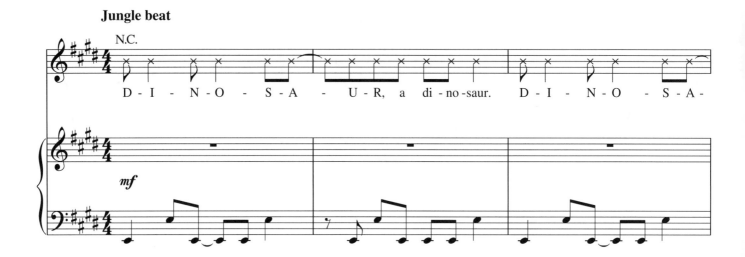

D-I-N-O-S-A-U-R, a di-no-saur. D-I-N-O-S-A-

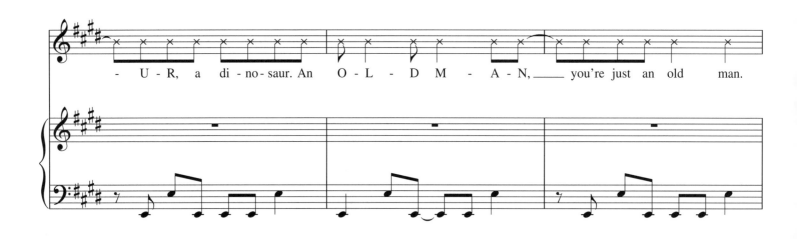

-U-R, a di-no-saur. An O-L-D-M-A-N,___ you're just an old man.

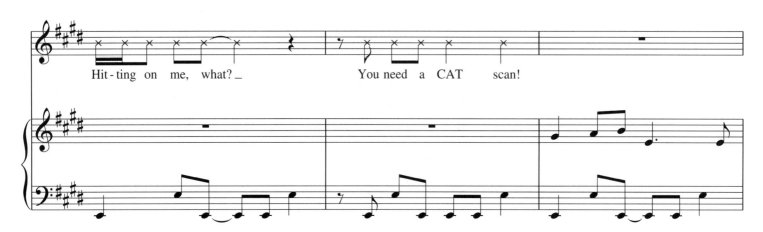

Hit-ting on me, what?___ You need a CAT scan!

Old man,____ why are you star - ing at me? Mack __
Not long _____ 'til you're _____ a sen - ior cit - i - zen and

____ on me _____ and my friends, ___ it's kind of creep - y.
you can strut a - round with your sex - y tank of ox - y - gen.

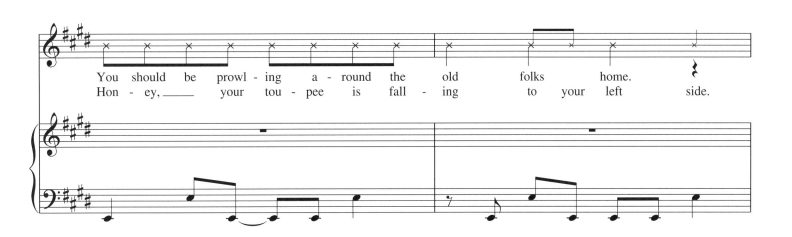

You should be prowl - ing a - round the old folks home.
Hon - ey, ____ your tou - pee is fall - ing to your left side.

DANCING WITH TEARS IN MY EYES

Words and Music by KESHA SEBERT,
LUKASZ GOTTWALD, BENJAMIN LEVIN
and CLAUDE KELLY

Pop Rock

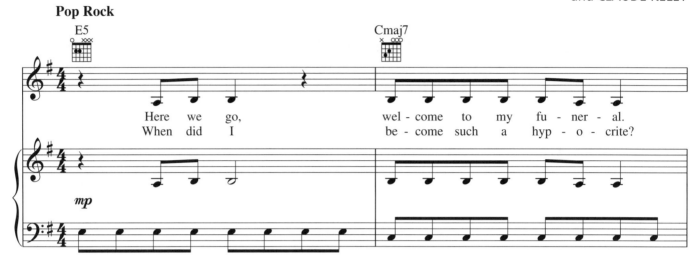

Here we go, wel-come to my fu-ner-al.
When did I be-come such a hyp-o-crite?

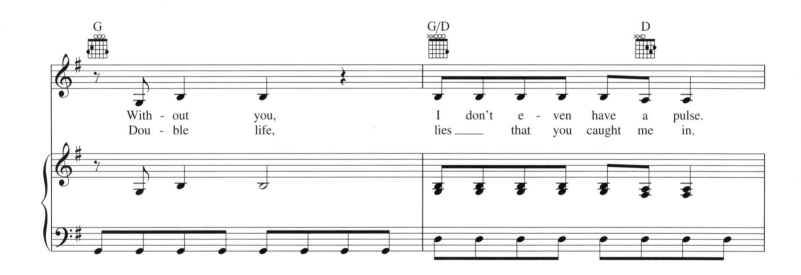

With-out you, I don't e-ven have a pulse.
Dou-ble life, lies____ that you caught me in.

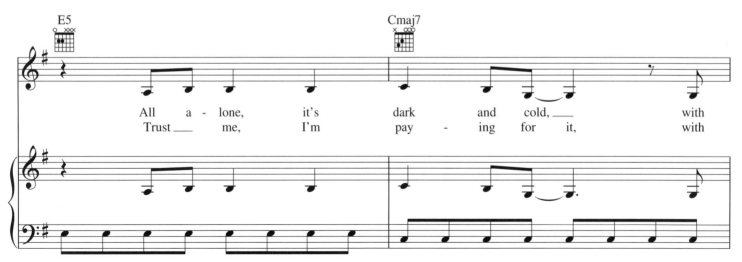

All a-lone, it's dark and cold,____ with
Trust____ me, I'm pay-ing for it, with

BOOTS & BOYS

Words and Music by KESHA SEBERT,
OLIVIA NERVO, MIRIAM NERVO
and TOM NEVILLE

With energy

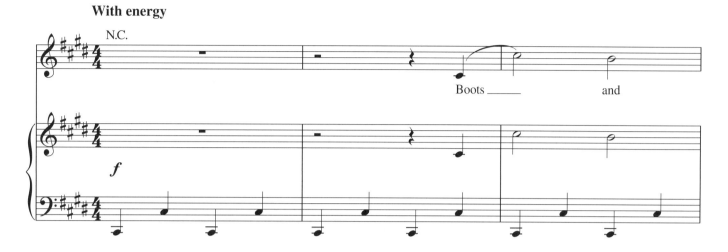

ANIMAL

Words and Music by KESHA SEBERT,
LUKASZ GOTTWALD, PEBE SEBERT
and GREG KURSTIN

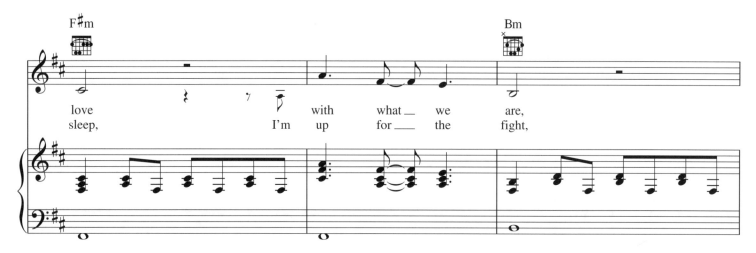

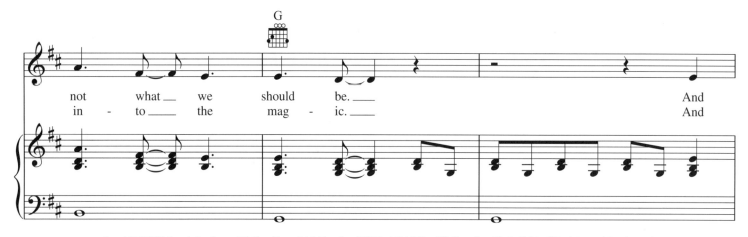

let it live,___ then die.___

Like it's the end___ of time,___

like ev - 'ry - thing ___ in - side, ___

let it live ___ and die. ___ This is ___ our

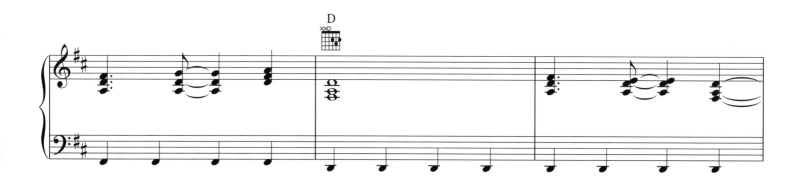

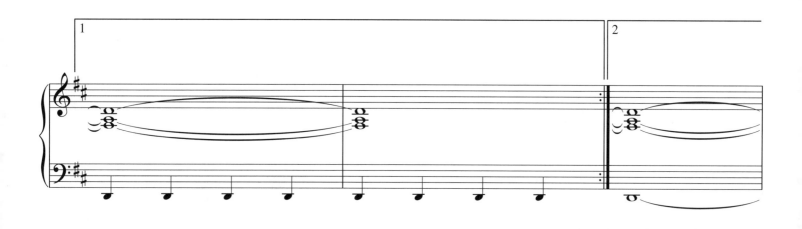

This is ___ our last _____ chance. ___ Give me

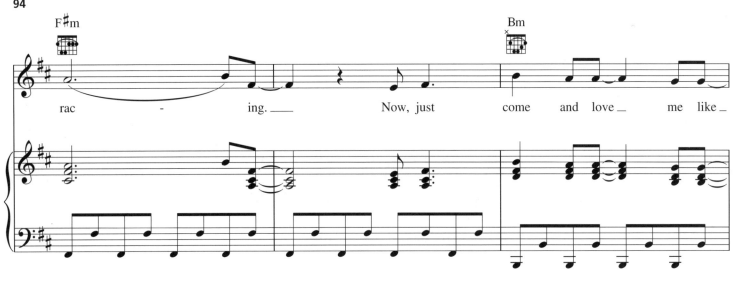

rac - ing. ___ Now, just come and love ___ me like ___

___ we're gon - na die. ___ Oh. ___

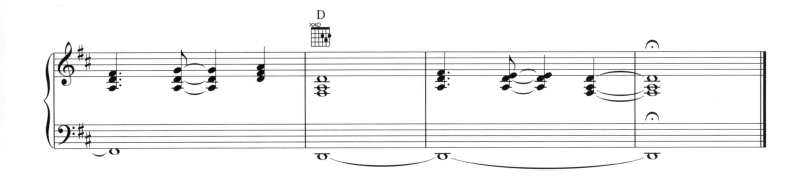